AF413305

Sacred Fossil Chronicles

Sacred Fossil Chronicles

Matthew Petchinsky

Sacred Fossil Chronicles: Blank Journal
By: Matthew Petchinsky